# MEMORY OF A GOLDFISH

# MEMORY OF A GOLDFISH

Katherine King

Copyright © 2025 Katherine King

All rights reserved

The characters and events portrayed in this book are fictitious. Any similarity to real persons, living or dead, is coincidental and not intended by the author.

No part of this book may be reproduced, or stored in a retrieval system, or transmitted in any form or by any means, electronic, mechanical, photocopying, recording, or otherwise, without express written permission of the publisher.

ISBN: 979-8-218-72937-0

Printed in the United States of America

Self Published

# AUTHOR'S NOTE

I didn't write this to be understood
I wrote it because
it's lived in me for too long.

because no one noticed when I went quiet
because I kept making myself smaller
and still called it love.

these words are what's left
after everyone took what they needed
and left without looking back.

they called me loud
that I talked too much
and cared too fast.

I started shrinking
before I ever had the chance to bloom.

I became the quietest in the room
not because I wanted too
but they told me time
and time again
to be quiet.

## MEMORY OF A GOLDFISH

the hardest part
isn't that they left.

it's that they never asked
why I was drowning.

they just called me dramatic
for gasping.

I handed out softness
like it cost nothing.

but it did
it cost me everything
it cost me
*me.*

## MEMORY OF A GOLDFISH

I reached out
no one reached back
and that's when I knew
it was never about me
only what I gave.

I became
the safe place
the steady ground
the one who never asked for help
but knew how to give it.

people came to me
to spill
to fall apart
to rest
and I let them.

because I love
I thought that was love
because I didn't know
no one would hold me.

## MEMORY OF A GOLDFISH

I forgot what I wanted
before I ever got the chance
to want it.

I shared myself
around what everyone
else needed
and called it
purpose.

I've always been the strong one
the listener
the calm
the fixer
the container.

I made space
for everyone else's grief
even when I was drowning
in my own.

I learned to nod
to soothe
to shrink
so others could breathe.

no one ever asked
what it cost me
to hold all that weight
with no hands to catch me
when I finally collapsed.

## MEMORY OF A GOLDFISH

a thread
I didn't mean to pull
found its way
through every seam.

nothing unraveled
not fully.

but some things
never quite smoothed
back into place.

being everything for everyone
meant being nothing for me.

## MEMORY OF A GOLDFISH

I cried in the car
with the volume high enough
to drown the ache.

I texted people
who never loved me back
I smiled at work
then broke down
alone in the parking lot.

no one noticed.

I wanted to scream
*I'm* not okay
I'm *not* okay
I'm not *okay*.

but instead
I told myself
to get up
because no one
was coming.

## MEMORY OF A GOLDFISH

they didn't slam a door
or shout a final word
they took longer to reply
until the silence felt polite.

I watched the dots fade
and knew
they chose to leave.

my heartbreak is a dress
two sizes too small
it pinches when I breathe
but no one mentions that
they just compliment the color.

## MEMORY OF A GOLDFISH

I took a different way home once
just to see where it led
it wasn't shorter
it wasn't easier
but the light hit different
through the trees.

you stopped texting back
you would change the subject
every time I tried to open up
it was clear I was too much.

I thought you'd be with me forever
you knew every version of me
until you decided this one
wasn't worth staying for.

## MEMORY OF A GOLDFISH

nobody asked why my eyes were empty
nobody noticed the crack in my voice
nobody saw the girl inside of me
begging for someone
to call it what it was.

## KATHERINE KING

I used to be a lighthouse
now I'm the plank that broke off the dock
bobbing alone in black water
waiting for land
that will never come.

## MEMORY OF A GOLDFISH

I thought if I could be better
quieter
softer
easier
they would want to stay.

turns out
it was just as easy
for them to leave.

I never wanted to be a sad story
never wanted to be someone
people looked at with soft eyes
and quiet pity.

but here I am
silently
with more cracks
then I used to have
and less people that love me
then before.

## MEMORY OF A GOLDFISH

I didn't just lose friends
I lost witnesses
people who knew me
full of color.

now there is no one left
who remembers the way
I used to laugh.

I gave them my light
thinking they'd glow beside me
thinking love meant offering
the brightest parts of me.

but they used it
to burn me
to warm themselves
while I faded.

and when there was nothing left
they called me
too dim
as if they hadn't stolen it.

## MEMORY OF A GOLDFISH

the sun doesn't wait to be welcomed
it just shows up every morning
pouring light onto the coldest corners
warming things it will never directly touch.

it keeps rising
even when no one is watching
even when the world keeps spinning
and people curse its heat
or take its light for granted.

I think there's something sacred about that
about the way I keep showing up for people
who don't even know I'm the reason they're not frozen.

and yet
I so often sit in the shadows alone
no one ever wonders
what keeps *me* burning.

you made me laugh
when my mouth had forgotten how.

you looked at me like you knew
who was supposed to be under there.

and for the first time
I believed it.

you didn't save me
you didn't need too.

you reminded me
my light still existed.

## MEMORY OF A GOLDFISH

I didn't want sympathy
I just wanted
someone to stay.

to look at my unraveling
and say
I'm not going anywhere.

and no one did.

before I miss anyone else
I miss me.

the girl who danced in the car
believed in love
in friendships
in herself.

I don't know when she left
but I hope she comes back.

## MEMORY OF A GOLDFISH

there was a moment today
that was just so ridiculous
you would've hated it
or maybe loved it too much.

I smiled
like I was sharing it with you
but the space between us
kept me quiet.

you were a gift
not a gift that stays
but the kind that shows up.

soft and brief
and changes everything
without even trying.

## MEMORY OF A GOLDFISH

there were days
I didn't even recognize myself.

the way I spoke so gently to others
but tore myself apart in silence
the way I poured love
into people who didn't return it
the way I smiled and said *It's fine*
while breaking in places
no one even looked at.

I didn't need saving
I needed someone to notice
and when no one did
I had to choose myself
out of sheer survival
not out of strength.

out of exhaustion.

your presence felt
like safety
in a world that stopped
being safe.

## MEMORY OF A GOLDFISH

they asked if I was okay
I said yes
they smiled
and I hated them
for believing me.

your silence used to feel like punishment
like something I had to earn
like maybe if I'd said one more thing
or said it differently
you'd still be here.

now it feels more like weather
always present
always shifting
sometimes it settles around me like fog
sometimes it leaves room for sun.

either way
I don't expect you to come back
when the clouds clear.

## MEMORY OF A GOLDFISH

if sadness marked the skin
in violet blooms and blackened rings
maybe they would've stayed
maybe they would've loved me
through the ache.

but when my body
matched my heart
they turned their backs
as if bleeding
was a choice.

after you left
I missed you
in the quiet places
where your voice
used to echo.

not in my ears
but in my chest.

## MEMORY OF A GOLDFISH

I wanted to be soft
but life made me sharp
then people left
because I wasn't
easy anymore.

the forest is layered with loss
fallen branches and crumbled bark
leaves that once reached for the sun
now pressed into the dirt
and yet it's not a graveyard.

that's the part people forget
nothing is wasted
nothing is useless
the decay is what makes
the roots stronger.

I think I've lived there most of my life
carrying pieces of who I used to be
and pieces of what I've given away.

I've been the leaves that were used and discarded
I've been the roots ignored
while everyone admired the shade.

but I've also been the soil
I've held things together long after they fell apart
I've nourished others while starving quietly.

the soil holds memory
the roots hold strength
and I carry both in silence.

## MEMORY OF A GOLDFISH

I lived
on scraps of affection
and called it
a feast.

one day I stopped crying to you
not because I was healed
because I stopped expecting
anyone to care.

the silence after the storm
wasn't peaceful
it was my punishment.

because now
I could hear everything
I tried to ignore.

our timing was wrong
at least that's what I've said
but maybe not.

maybe you were meant
to walk through my life
exactly when you did.

## MEMORY OF A GOLDFISH

I knew I would always
become the person
that I once needed.

I meant that I'd
shape myself
with purpose.

to listen without judgement
to see the silent pain
but I didn't know
I'd still be the one
whispering get up
to myself.

silently
and
alone.

you never said goodbye
and I never
stopped listening for it.

## MEMORY OF A GOLDFISH

I stopped texting first
I stopped oversharing
stopped chasing people
who didn't hold space for me.

the loneliness was sharp at first
now it's a room I live in
without even flinching.

I am made
of what everyone
left behind.

the gifts no one claimed
the stories no one asked about
the pain I tucked away.

I've always hated leftovers.

## MEMORY OF A GOLDFISH

when I hear a joke
my first instinct
is to send it to you.

I don't
but the instinct
says enough.

they loved the version
I bled to create.

## MEMORY OF A GOLDFISH

I say I'm done
I say I hate them
and I say it again
and again
like if I repeat it enough
it might be true.

so many goodbyes
that never happened.

so many people
who faded
without explanation.

I've had to write closure
over and over again.

## MEMORY OF A GOLDFISH

I used to speak with color
now everything comes out grey.

some endings come
with flowers and farewells.

others
come quietly
and leave you wondering
if they were ever real.

I've buried more
than anyone knows
and mourned in silence
because there was no grave
to stand beside.

## MEMORY OF A GOLDFISH

when the chaos ended
I thought I'd feel calm
but all that came
was a noise
only I could hear.

my own voice
echoing
what now
who am I
without the storm?

## KATHERINE KING

I spent years
existing for others
being palatable
being useful
being easy.

being whatever version
they wanted.

the silence began
and I met the echo
of someone
I didn't recognize.

## MEMORY OF A GOLDFISH

I
bent
until
you
forgot
I
could
stand.

you made all the sense
in the world
like finding a key
to a door I didn't know existed.

but you made no sense at all
like a riddle
I couldn't quite solve
a puzzle missing a piece
that kept me searching.

you were both the calm
and the storm
the answer
and the question
and somehow
I didn't want it any other way.

## MEMORY OF A GOLDFISH

how do you say
you don't want to exist
not like this
not with all this ache
I just want to feel
anything other than pain.

I don't tell people anymore
I stopped explaining myself
people will only hear
what they want to hear.

they forgive
only what they can relate too.
they bend the truth
when it suits them.

now I just nod
and smile
I keep the mess
to myself.

## MEMORY OF A GOLDFISH

I am grieving
not just the people
but the versions of me
that trusted too fast
loved too hard
believed too easily
and never asked for more.

I am grieving the girl
I outgrew
and the life
I thought would save me.

## KATHERINE KING

I caught a joke
in the corner of my mind
something you'd roll your eyes at
or maybe laugh too loud for.

I wanted to tell you
but the words
got stuck
between my lips and the silence.

## MEMORY OF A GOLDFISH

I'm not hard to love
just done begging
for scraps of it.

if our paths never cross again
I'll still believe
that something in the universe
allowed our souls to bump shoulders.

just long enough
to remind me
how rare it is
to feel so known
by someone you just met.

I hope we meet again
in every version of this life
and the next.

## MEMORY OF A GOLDFISH

sometimes I question
if I imagined her
the version of me
who smiled easier
breathed deeper
felt safe in her own skin.

but she was real
and just because you're gone
doesn't mean she has to be.

I laughed different with you
not the polite laugh
the real kind
the one I forgot I had.

## MEMORY OF A GOLDFISH

I've always been the clever girl
the one who could read between the silences
rewrite endings before they began.

but clever doesn't save you
when you love the *idea* of someone
more than who they really are.

## KATHERINE KING

I don't regret you
I've made a lot of mistakes
but you weren't one of them.

you were breath
you were light
you were warmth
in the coldest parts of my life.

I don't regret you
I regret not having more time
with the version of me
you brought back.

## MEMORY OF A GOLDFISH

there's a small group
a handful of souls
whose laughter still echoes
in the corners of my mind
where it settles
soft and strange
like a song I almost remember
but can't quite sing.

I miss the way
their laughter fit mine
like puzzle pieces
forgotten in a box
now closed
sealed
and gone.

and the strangest part is
knowing they won't come back
the silence between us
isn't waiting to be filled
it's just empty.

even when we don't talk
even when the days
turn into years
you're still the one
my heart finds
when everything else
gets too loud.

## MEMORY OF A GOLDFISH

thank you
for believing in me
when even I
wasn't sure I could.

thank you
for challenging me
to rise higher
than my own doubts allowed.

thank you
for trusting me
with your time
your truth.

thank you
for empowering me
to find my own voice
even when it trembled.

thank you
for seeing me
the parts I tried to hide
the parts I was afraid to love.

thank you
for caring
without conditions
without expecting anything back.

thank you
for being the light
that helped me
find my own.

you might not stay
in this lifetime.

but I believe
our souls
have already promised
to find each other.

again
and
again.

## MEMORY OF A GOLDFISH

I don't believe
in coincidences.

not the places I've landed
not the people who crossed my path
even the ones
who didn't stay.

some broke me
some built me
some just held the mirror
long enough
for me to see myself clearly.

and none of it was by accident.

they only called it anger
because it was louder
than my silence.

the forest doesn't ask to be witnessed
it just grows
quietly and relentlessly

it sheds and sprouts and reaches
even when no one's watching.

there are trees that have stood
longer than love has lasted
moss that softens stone
without needing a single soul to notice
and still it gives.

I think I am like that
steady
generous
uncelebrated
loving without needing applause.

but some days
it would be nice to be the wildflower
someone stops for
not because they need
something from me
but because they finally *see* the way
I've been blooming all along.

I hate that they
made me question
my joy
my light
my willingness to give people
the benefit of the doubt.

I hate that they
made me second guess
the way I show up for people
like maybe that's why they leave.

like maybe if I was
colder
quieter
more detached
they'd respect me more.

but why should I have to
become smaller to be loved right
why do I have to dim myself
to keep people around?

I'd rather be left
than become someone
I'm not.

## MEMORY OF A GOLDFISH

I will search for pieces of you
in every person I meet
not to replace you
but because I miss you.

I'll keep my chin up
like I promised I would.

never again.

I will never be
that version of me.

who begged
someone to stay.

## MEMORY OF A GOLDFISH

a single leaf falls
not because the wind pushed it
but because it was ready to let go
it's spins in circles
dances before it rests.

sometimes I think about how that feels
to choose the fall
instead of being torn apart .

my eyes have studied
absence like scripture.

they've watched people
walk away mid sentence
watched doors close
with no goodbye.

watched love shift
slowly into distance
until even the light
in the room felt different.

they've searched for
signs that weren't there
scanned every silence
for hidden meaning.

and sometimes
when I look in the mirror
I don't even recognize them
not because they've changed
but because they finally
stopped hoping
they stopped asking
to be seen.

they just watch now
like windows in a house
no one visits anymore.

## MEMORY OF A GOLDFISH

it's my first time living
maybe I'll get it wrong
and maybe I already have.

but how else do you learn
what you really want
unless you stop being
who they told you to be?

if I spoke the truth
they'd turn away
call it dramatic
call me selfish.

but they weren't the ones
lying awake at night
feeling more gone than alive.

so they don't get to judge
how I crawled
out of it.

## MEMORY OF A GOLDFISH

it's humbling
when all I want is to spill
the weight off my chest
to word vomit
into someone's open arms.

but there is no one there.

so I swallow it whole
bury it deep
tell myself to get up
wipe away the tears
slow my breath back to calm
and carry on with the day.

the worst kind of pain
isn't the kind that comes
from being left.

it's the kind that comes
from realizing
you lost yourself
while trying to keep
someone else.

## MEMORY OF A GOLDFISH

my absence isn't affecting you
I thought I mattered more than silence
I thought leaving would echo
would rattle something in you
the way your leaving unraveled me.

you move like I was never there
and I sit with that
not because I want you back
but because I wanted to mean something
even when I had to walk away.

I deserved more
than the silence it lived in.

## MEMORY OF A GOLDFISH

my body remembers
the ache isn't just in my chest.

it lives in my bones
my jaw
my stomach
my hands.

my body remembers
what it felt like to be left behind.

when all I wanted to do
was beg you to stay.

you let me go so easily
like it was nothing
and maybe it was.

but I lost sleep
protecting your peace.

I wasn't perfect
but I tried.

and all that trying
left me with regret.

## MEMORY OF A GOLDFISH

I don't know how to explain
what it feels like
to give someone all your softness
only to watch them walk away
carrying all of it.

there's a part of the forest no light touches
a place deep beneath the canopy where things rot
and yet somehow
life still begins again.

that's where I live
in the quiet decay
in the soft dark spaces
where old things fall apart
and feed what's next.

people love the trees that bloom
the obvious beauty
the ones in spring.

but me?

I've lived enough lives in silence
to know that the real transformation
doesn't happen where it's bright.

it happens where no one is watching
where things break down
where old roots surrender
so new ones can grow.

and maybe that's why no one sees me clearly
because the most important parts of me
are unfolding in the dark
where they stopped looking.

## MEMORY OF A GOLDFISH

I believed you
your eyes and your voice
and the way you leaned in.

but you always left
each time I knew you would come back
And I knew I would let you.

maybe that makes me naïve
but what does that make you?

maybe you never meant it
maybe you were just playing a part
maybe you knew how to play it well
but I didn't.

I meant every word
every glance
every beat of my heart
that moved towards you.

## MEMORY OF A GOLDFISH

this version of me
was built
with bruises and boundaries
with grief and grace.

I was the loud one once
the chatterbox filling rooms with my voice
I used to think connection
was as simple as sharing pieces of myself.

but the world made me smaller
a look when I talked too long
a friend who drifted when I got hard to hold
a silence when there should have been softness.

I stopped speaking unless I was invited
I only told stories when they asked me twice
They want the easy version of me
the one who laughs
and who loves without question.

but i'm still here
still full of things I haven't said in years
still holding stories I never told.

I guess I keep forgetting
that not everyone loves like I do
that not everyone knows what it means
to give without measure.

so I keep giving
not because I'm weak
not because I'm hoping for something in return
but because it's who I've always been.

some days I wonder if that's all I was made for
to hold everyone else's pain
to be the place they plant their mess and move on from.

and even then
I hope they grow.

## MEMORY OF A GOLDFISH

the hardest part
is knowing I can't even tell you
how much it hurts
how much I still carry
how much I still wonder.

you moved on
and I stayed behind
with all the questions
we didn't have time to answer.

there's something about a wildfire
they never tell you
it doesn't just destroy
it *clears*.

it strips things down to the bones
it forces truth
it makes space.

and after the flames
something miraculous happens
certain seeds
ones that have laid dormant for years
*only* open in fire.

I think about that a lot
about how maybe
I wasn't ruined by what hurt me
maybe I was *activated*.

maybe the pain didn't break me down
but cracked me open
because after everything burned
I began to see myself clearer.

and maybe that's what love is supposed to be
not the thing that keeps you untouched
but the thing that sets you on fire
and teaches you who you are
when the smoke finally clears.

## MEMORY OF A GOLDFISH

I don't believe
we just meet people
we are sent
to each other.

## KATHERINE KING

bruises don't always bloom right away
they arrive quiet
a shadow beneath the skin
before it remembers how to ache.

someone brushes against you
and you flinch
not because it hurt
but because it reminded your body
that it had been hurt before.

I have bruises like that
some are purple, yellow, green
proof I bumped into the wrong things
held on too tightly
tried to carry something I shouldn't have.

but most of them you won't find
they live in places where skin can't swell
in my voice where I learned to stay quiet
in my back where I bent too far for someone
in the space behind my ribs
where I tucked the apology I never got.

and still
I move gently through the world
not because I've forgotten the bruises
but because I've learned where not to press.

## MEMORY OF A GOLDFISH

no one can judge
no one will ever know
the whole story.

not what I carried
not what I survived
not what it cost me.

to finally choose me.

my hands are always full.

they've packed boxes
no one helped carry
written apologies I didn't owe
clutched the steering wheel
while crying so hard
I couldn't see straight.

they've picked up the phone
reached across silence
they've clung to people
who were already halfway gone.

and still they stay open
but not without trembling
because no one taught them
how to be cared for
without first being useful.

and I wonder when they'll learn
that being empty
doesn't mean they failed
only that they gave without question
like they always do.

## MEMORY OF A GOLDFISH

My eyes have memorized
the look people give
right before they
decide to stop loving you.

they have watched
laughter leave a room
and silence settle
in like dust.

they have searched
faces for softness
and learned to live
with the cold instead.

I've learned
to swallow the storm
before it ever
reaches the surface.

but if you look
long enough
you will see
the exhaustion
the private kind
the kind that can't be fixed
only witnessed.

## MEMORY OF A GOLDFISH

I used to think
I loved her laugh
because it was joy
but now I know
it was armor.

every joke
was a deflection
every punchline was a way
to keep the world from noticing
how tired she really was.

scars are strange things
even the smallest cut
accidental and forgotten
can leave its mark
long after the pain has gone quiet.

some of mine are visible
I know exactly where they came from
I know the color of the night
the sharpness of the word
the way I stood there
and didn't flinch until later.

others are less precise
they appeared when I stopped speaking
when I stopped being believed
when I kept choosing to stay
even after I knew I shouldn't.

they don't fade the way people promise
but they do teach you
the shape of your own survival.

## MEMORY OF A GOLDFISH

I don't know how to be halfway
I don't know how to care casually
I don't know how to love in moderation.

and maybe that's
always been my problem
that I give everything
before being asked.

and when it doesn't work out
I don't stop loving them
I just carry it quietly
like a weight I chose
even though I never meant to.

I'm not angry that they left
I'm angry that I stayed
long after I knew they would.

that I explained
myself one more time
thinking maybe this time
they'd understand
that I made their comfort
more important
than my clarity.

that I loved them
past the end
because I don't know how
to be the one who leaves.

## MEMORY OF A GOLDFISH

I miss being soft
without fear
I miss saying what I feel
without wondering
if it'll scare someone off.

I used to speak
from the heart
and trust that it would
land in safe hands.

now I speak carefully
I measure my tone
I wonder if too much of me
is something people leave over.

and even now
I still hope one day
i'll meet someone
who doesn't make me
feel like I have to shrink.

I know how to disappear gracefully
you won't hear a slammed door
you won't get a bitter text
you'll just stop hearing from me.

because when I finally leave
I've already forgiven you
for not being who I needed
I've already stopped waiting
for you to notice I was hurting.

I've already said goodbye
a hundred times
in the silence
between your lack of effort
and my quiet hope
that maybe this time
you'd show up differently.

## MEMORY OF A GOLDFISH

I reached out
no one reached back
and that's when I knew
it was never about me
only what I gave.

## KATHERINE KING

I don't regret loving you
even though it hurt
even though it changed me.

I'd still do it again
not to change the ending
but because you saw me.

maybe not forever
maybe not clearly
but for a moment
you saw my light.

and even if you're the one
who dimmed it
I'm glad you knew it was there
and that it was mine.

## MEMORY OF A GOLDFISH

To them my eyes are just
green and steady
eyes people said were kind
the kind that listened
the kind that forgave
before they're asked to.

but what they really saw
was comfort in my gaze
not the weight I carried
not the things I saw.

they never really knew me
they just liked how it felt
to be known by me.

## MEMORY OF A GOLDFISH

I've always been the one
who stays too long
who holds on past
the point of comfort
who waits for a sign
that doesn't come.

I don't do it
out of weakness
I do it because
I believe in people
even when they've
stopped believing in me.

that's the part I haven't
learned to undo
the part that still loves
even after everything.

the dishes in the sink
have grown roots
I water them with my guilt
I watch the mold rise
like it's trying to become something
it's still more alive
than I've felt in weeks.

## MEMORY OF A GOLDFISH

I shared my memories
like photo albums spread out on the floor.

here's why I flinch at loud voices
here's why I laugh in silence
here's why I give so much.

I handed them the map to my becoming
and hoped they'd stay long enough
to understand the terrain.

I don't cry anymore
not because I'm healed
but because even the sadness
has gone still.

like old fruit
left too long on the counter
not sweet, not sour
just… soft.

just done.

## MEMORY OF A GOLDFISH

the bed has shaped itself around me
it knows my weight
too well now.

knows the side I turn to
when the ache feels louder
knows how long I'll stay
without moving.

the sheets don't smell like me anymore
they smell like stillness
like fabric that's forgotten
what air feels like.

I think the mattress is rotting with me
I think we made a pact
stay here
until we become one.

## KATHERINE KING

I don't regret what I said
but I regret who I said it to
they weren't listening
they were collecting
little pieces of me
to one day use as reasons
for why they left.

## MEMORY OF A GOLDFISH

oh how odd it is
that I showed you my heart
I gave you my light
made you a home deep inside my soul.

and still you robbed me
while I was willingly offering
you everything without hesitation
you didn't need to steal
what was already yours
what I gave freely
what lived inside me
long before you came.

how strange to be treated that way
when you knew you were just going to be
another shadow in a line of others
who already did the same.

I screamed the same song in the car
three times in a row
not because I liked it
but because it understood.

because when the chorus hit
and my voice cracked trying to match it
I felt something shake loose
pain maybe
hope maybe
I don't know.

but for a minute
I wasn't numb
for a minute
I was alive.

## MEMORY OF A GOLDFISH

I overexpose
like film left in the sun
not because I want attention
but because silence
feels more suffocating
than being misunderstood.

I showed my heart
but not like in a museum
it wasn't something protected by glass
wasn't framed with velvet ropes and warning signs
it was open
and accessible
it was there to be touched
and most people did
not to admire it
but to see what it could give them
and how quickly they could walk away after.

## MEMORY OF A GOLDFISH

I used to wait
hoping someone would notice
would ask
would reach.

but they never did
and so
like every time before
I wipe my own tears
stand on tired legs
and carry myself
through the storm
no one even saw.

I wonder if they're haunted
the way I am
if something ever catches them off guard
like my laugh in a stranger
or a joke only we ever understood.

do they feel the silence
do they notice my absence
in places I used to fill.

I've stopped hoping
but not wondering
those are two different things.

## MEMORY OF A GOLDFISH

I'm not quieter
Because I'm ashamed
I'm quieter
because I've learned
not everyone knows
how to hold a story
without twisting it.

I give myself permission
to want what I want
to feel what I feel
to make a mess
and clean it up
without shame.

this is growth
this is grace
this is mine.

## MEMORY OF A GOLDFISH

no one saw the unanswered texts
waiting quietly in my phone
and if they did
they said nothing.

no one noticed
when I shut the door
on the people I love
and if they did
they held their silence.

they heard me say *I'm tired*
but didn't notice
I never explained why.

## KATHERINE KING

I'm not sorry for what I said
I'm not sorry for what I felt
I'm not sorry for the way I reached.

I needed to know
what it felt like
to choose myself
just once.

## MEMORY OF A GOLDFISH

some people
were lessons.

some people
were maps.

all of them
were meant.

## KATHERINE KING

I didn't think about
the second fall
the one that comes
after you've already healed
already crawled your way back
already become someone
you were proud of.

and then something shatters again
and no one's there
and you realize
it's lonelier now
because you knew better
you thought you were done falling.

## MEMORY OF A GOLDFISH

I look back sometimes
not to dwell
just to remind myself
even the worst days
placed me somewhere better.

none of it
was wasted
every wound
every word
every goodbye
it all happened
on purpose.

I stopped being the quiet one
stopped pleasing everyone
and started listening
to what my body
was screaming for
and what my heart
was begging for.

it looked messy
because it was
but it also looked honest.

## MEMORY OF A GOLDFISH

I spent years
carrying pain that wasn't mine
making myself small
so others could feel big.

now I stretch
breathe deeper
take up the space
I've always deserved.

this time
I don't want the chaos
the confusion
the convincing.

I want
a heart
that feels
like home.

and if I don't
find it here
I will build it
myself.

## MEMORY OF A GOLDFISH

I let it all burn
because sometimes healing
looks like destruction.

letting what once was fall apart
letting the pieces find their own place
letting the silence speak for itself.

I knew it would hurt
to let it all burn
but I had to.

one day
I caught myself laughing again
not forced
not for show
the real kind.

the kind that feels like
coming home.

and I thought of you
because that was yours
that was the part of me
you brought back.

## MEMORY OF A GOLDFISH

I wasn't healing yet
just drifting
not drowning
but not reaching for shore.

I was somewhere
in between
giving up
and starting over.

there's no shame
in starting over
in getting it wrong
in learning the hard way.

the process
is the point
and the progress
is the proof.

## MEMORY OF A GOLDFISH

I used to think
I was behind
like I missed something
like life was waiting for me
to catch up.

but now I know
every late start
every closed door
every wrong turn
brought me here.

I wasn't late
I was right on time.

my healing isn't linear
my boundaries wobble
my joy is quiet
not constant.

but I'm proud
of this mess
even if I made it.

it is mine
it is honest
and it is earned.

## MEMORY OF A GOLDFISH

I have tested my limits
I don't regret it
I regret how long I lived
for everyone else's approval.

somehow
I became the girl
who followed every rule
kept her head down
asked to speak
before she spoke.

until one day
I realized
I was obeying a life
that didn't fit me.

I've always followed my own rules
my head never bowed
I spoke often
and too truthfully
for their comfort.

I will never return
to the version of me
that stayed silent
so they could stay comfortable.

## MEMORY OF A GOLDFISH

healing is not a race
there's not a finish line
waiting for me at the end
it's a slow unfolding of a flower
petal by petal
sometimes bruised
sometimes bright
learning to bloom again
in its own imperfect time.

I'm learning that choosing yourself
doesn't always look like
loud declarations or big decisions.

sometimes it looks like
saying the truth
and not apologizing for how it made them feel.

sometimes it looks like
laughing out loud again
like really loud
without shrinking.

it looks like taking up space
in your own life
like sitting alone at dinner
and not feeling like you're waiting for someone.

like speaking
even when your voice shakes
like keeping the boundaries
even when they push back.

I used to think choosing myself
would feel selfish
but it feels like *peace*.

it feels like coming home
and this time
I'm not waiting
for someone to meet me there.

## MEMORY OF A GOLDFISH

the plants in her windowsill
began to bend with her
leaves curling inward
like they were trying to hold onto something
they could not name.

some days the sun poured in
and they reached for it
bold and openly
as if they believed in warmth again.

other days
they slouched in their pots
parched and quiet
sensing the heaviness in the room
without needing a reason.

they didn't need language
to understand her
they just mirrored her silence
her slow forgetting
and her soft return.

I am still me
still thoughtful
still soft
still loving
all in ways most people don't notice
until it's gone.

but not for the ones that I told I was struggling
not for the ones who looked at my breaking
and chose silence
who stepped back
when I need them to step in
who disappeared
while I was losing pieces of myself.

you're lucky I already knew
how to hold myself together
without the people I used to call home
lucky I didn't let your absence
become the reason I disappeared too.

the trees stand steady
not because they don't sway
but because they've learned to bend
with the weight of the wind
to hold their roots deep in the dark earth
while the storm washes over them.

sometimes I think of them
when the world feels too heavy
and I wonder if I
could be that strong
that patient
if I could learn to hold myself
through the storms.

but then I remember
I already did.

closure is a myth
we chase to feel better
about people who never cared
enough to explain.

how silly
that we look for an answer
from someone
who chose to disappear.

## MEMORY OF A GOLDFISH

you can keep the explanations
the long text and the guilt
I've made peace with the version of you
that never showed up
and I've made peace with the version of me
that still wanted you too.

I don't have to apologize
for days when the shadows win
for moments when the tears fall easy.

because healing isn't about perfection to me
it's about kindness to myself
even when the pieces don't fit yet.

## MEMORY OF A GOLDFISH

healing didn't teach me
to close off
it taught me
to guard the door.

to let love in
but not anyone
who just wants to peek around
and leave their shoes on my floor.

I don't need your reasons
I don't need the carefully worded apology
that you'll never send.

I stopped rehearsing what I'd say
if you came back
you lost access to that version of me
the one who needed answers
and the one who waited.

I'm not her anymore.

## MEMORY OF A GOLDFISH

there are days now
where I laugh before noon
sing in the car with the windows down
forget to check my phone
because I'm too busy living.

healing didn't erase the pain
but it gave me this
a full breath
a soft morning
and a version of me
that finally feels like home.

I go to bed
without running
conversations in my head
and that feels like a miracle.

## MEMORY OF A GOLDFISH

sometimes the road makes no sense
until years later
when you're standing somewhere
you never meant to be
but somehow
feels like exactly
where you were headed all along.

## KATHERINE KING

I used to think I had to grow out of her
the one who talked too much
laughed too hard
loved with her whole chest.

but she's the best part of me
and no one
gets to dim that again
not even me.

## MEMORY OF A GOLDFISH

I still love deeply
but now I save some of it for myself.

I don't chase
I don't beg
I don't shrink.

and somehow
I'm more myself than I've ever been.

there's a softness in me again
not the kind that gets taken for granted
but the kind I fought to keep.

I feel like myself when I'm loud
when I'm teasing the people I love
when I'm dancing without music
just because the mood is right.

this isn't performative
this is peace.

## MEMORY OF A GOLDFISH

I missed her
the girl who lit up the room
without even trying
she's back now
and she's glowing.

for the first time in a long time
I'm not searching
for the version of me
I used to be
she's already here.

she's alive in the way
I throw my head back when I laugh
in the way
I take up space without apology
in the way
I no longer overthink how bright I shine.

## MEMORY OF A GOLDFISH

I don't pretend to be perfect
I've said the wrong things
stayed too long
loved people who didn't know
what to do with my heart.

but I never came with bad intentions
I never played games
I gave what I had
and sometimes more.

that doesn't make me weak
it makes me real
and if you mistook that
for something you could use
you'll never get that version of me again.

Yes I forgive easily
Yes I try to see the good
but don't confuse softness
with submission.

I've learned how
to protect my peace
without hardening my heart.

I still lead with love
I still give freely
but not to those who think
it's theirs to take.

## MEMORY OF A GOLDFISH

I burst out laughing
before the jokes even landed
and make the room
a little bit brighter just by being there
I am the kind of light
that makes others forget their shadows.

I'll keep showing up with love
that won't change
it's who I am
but I've stopped handing it to people
who only hold it long enough
to wring it out.

## MEMORY OF A GOLDFISH

you don't get to say I changed
when I stopped letting you hurt me
you don't get to miss my softness
when you were the reason
I built walls around it.

I still love big
I still give deep
but now I check
who's at the door
before I open it.

I love the way I think
the way I feel deeply
the way I notice what others don't
it's not too much
it's not dramatic
it's not naïve
it's *me.*

and I'm done pretending to be anything less
just to make others more comfortable.

## MEMORY OF A GOLDFISH

it's funny really
how everyone claimed to love me
when I was bright and laughing
when I made things easy
when I held all the weight without showing it.

then I crashed
and they all vanished
like I was never theirs to begin with.

now I'm back
and maybe they'll circle around again
maybe I'll smile
maybe I'll even hug them
but they'll never get close enough
to dim me twice.

I'm beautiful
not just in the way I look
though I've started to see that too
but in the way I carry myself
in the way I walk into a room
and bring it to life without even trying.

I used to hope
someone would tell me that
now I say it out loud
and mean it.

## MEMORY OF A GOLDFISH

I've rebuilt myself without them
that's the part they won't understand
that the girl who once waited for them to call
is the woman who doesn't care if they do.

don't confuse my joy with forgiveness
don't confuse this peace with an open door.

maybe they'll try to come back
now that I look like sunlight again
but they'll find the warmth
isn't free anymore.

## MEMORY OF A GOLDFISH

I've found myself again
maybe not all of me
but enough to stand tall
when the world tries to push me down.

I carry pieces of my past
but they don't define me anymore
I'm learning what it means
to hold space for myself
to guard my heart with kindness
and never let anyone walk over me again.

# STAY

I wrote through the heaviness
through the silence
through it all.

I am proud of the way I love
of the way I stayed soft
even when the world tried to harden me.

if you found yourself in these pages
I hope you know now
you don't have to shrink to survive.

stay bright
stay *you.*

# THANK YOU

to my family and friends
thank you for being steady
for loving me in the in-between
when I wasn't always easy to hold
your presence was a soft place
in a world that often felt too sharp.

to the ones who challenged me
misunderstood me
pushed me further
than I thought I could go
you gave me clarity.

this book holds all of it
all of you
and all the versions of me.

thank you.

www.ingramcontent.com/pod-product-compliance
Lightning Source LLC
Chambersburg PA
CBHW022107090426
42743CB00008B/754